THE SPIRIT OF

Edinburgh

THE SPIRIT OF
EDINBURGH

ROBIN WARD

RICHARD DREW PUBLISHING   GLASGOW

For Brian, Di and Lucy

Richard Drew Publishing Limited
6 Clairmont Gardens
Glasgow G3 7LW
Scotland

Half title: *Architectural detail in Princes Street*
Title page: *The city skyline looking west from Calton Hill*

Approaching Edinburgh on the Forth Railway Bridge

Ward, Robin
The Spirit of Edinburgh
1. Edinburgh (Lothian) – Description –
Guide-books
I. Title
914.13'404858   DA890.E3

ISBN 0 86267 131 0

Designed by Robin Ward
Photoset in Perpetua by Artwork Associates, Edinburgh and Glasgow
Colour separations by Intercrom SA, Madrid
Printed and bound by Blantyre Printing and Binding Company Limited, Blantyre

To arrive in Scotland's capital by train, or by taxi from the airport, through the city's amorphous suburbia and suddenly burst into the spacious arena that is the unbuilt side of Princes Street, is one of the great travel experiences of the world. But Edinburgh's city centre doesn't really look like a city centre. It's more like an 18th-century landscape garden which has grown completely out of control, as if the designer didn't know when to stop. It is a city centre of hills and wooded parkland, dotted with architectural curios and dominated by an ancient castle – a fairytale townscape.

Edinburgh today is a romantic and civilised capital, a popular tourist destination and a cosmopolitan cultural bazaar during the summer festival season. It is also a commercial capital, one of the richest financial centres in Europe. St Andrew Square is a veritable bevy of banks and insurance buildings. But this was not always so. Scotland's capital has a turbulent, bloody history; Edinburgh Castle, frequently fought over, was a major obstacle to any invasion of the country and the alleys of the Old Town were a haven for assassins and thieves – a dark undercurrent to the city's civilised veneer.

Edinburgh at times appears consumed by its history – Edwin Muir's 'handsome, empty capital of the past'. It has all the trappings of a true capital – a world famous arts festival, a parliament building, national museums and international financial interests – but it is a capital without a country, a ghostly stage set waiting for its performers to return. It has neither the metropolitan buzz nor (to Edinburgh ears) the vulgar self-confidence of its arch rival Glasgow. It is prim rather than pompous and cultivates an aloof certainty which can betray a deep-seated insecurity characteristic of Scots generally. Perversely, this factor usually reveals itself during the run-up to the Festival, the event which maintains Edinburgh's position on the world stage. Some local politicians once accused the Festival of bringing dissolute artists and performers to the city 'undermining the very fabric of society', but nowadays they level criticisms of élitism and threaten to dilute its status. However misguided some may be on this issue, recent politicians have begun to sweep Edinburgh clean of its image of cloying gentility which demographically is as false to the city as a whole as the cheerful Cockney is nowadays to London.

The 20th century seems at times to have passed Edinburgh by, but this is more a measure of the enduring quality of its monuments, history and people rather than any lack of progress in recent years. Edinburgh appears to achieve that delicate and desirable urban balance whereby its commerce and industry continues to prosper while the city's past is preserved. There are no skyscrapers or motorways in Edinburgh, although there was a 1960s plan (mercifully abandoned) to rebuild Princes Street as a sort of horizontal 'Alphaville'. There has been some regrettable redevelopment, notably on Edinburgh's University's campus and on the eastern periphery of the New Town where the St James Centre, possessed of no saintly qualities and looking as if it was imported 'en masse' from East Berlin, presides over the ruination of Leith Street's townscape.

Edinburgh's most visible asset is its townscape. No other city shows its social and topographic development as clearly or as dramatically as Edinburgh does – from the Castle and the medieval Old Town tumbling head-over-heels eastwards down its volcanic ridge to Holyrood Palace, to Princes Street and the elegant Georgian New Town, to the 19th and 20th-century suburbs which encircle the city centre.

The precipitous narrow streets of the Old Town and the dramatic perspectives of the New enthrall residents and visitors alike. There is a wonderful sense of space in Edinburgh. It is a city of panoramas, perspectives and sudden vistas – where turning a corner high up in the Old Town will unexpectedly reveal the city laid out below like a model-maker's dream. It is a vision which seems to have existed unchanged for centuries and is an historic backdrop giving consistency to Edinburgh's continuing, and potentially leading, role in Scotland's future.

Robin Ward, June 1985

Looking west from Calton Hill as dawn sunlight illuminates Edinburgh's dramatic central townscape:

From left to right: *The steeple (1829) of the 17th century Tron Kirk, framed by the columns of the Dugald Stewart Memorial built in 1832 on Calton Hill. Below in Calton Graveyard is the Martyrs' Monument obelisk and beyond, North Bridge leading up to the Old Town where the crowned tower of St Giles (1500), the steeple of Tolbooth St John's Church (1844) and Edinburgh Castle dominate the Royal Mile. In the background are the Pentland Hills.*

To the right of the Castle, in Princes Street, are the turn-of-the-century clock tower of the North British Hotel, the Scott Monument (1844), and the distant spires (1917) of St Mary's Episcopal Cathedral above the flat dome of Robert Adam's Register House (1811).

The classic view of Edinburgh's Old Town: The view east as the Royal Mile plunges towards Holyrood Palace showing the John Knox House jutting out into the High Street (the Royal Mile is a continuous thread of four streets, Castlehill, Lawnmarket, High Street and Canongate).

The John Knox House is named after the zealous 16th-century Scots reformer who played a prominent role in the Scottish Reformation of 1559-60, which resulted in the Scottish Parliament ending the authority of the Pope in the country and the creation of a Protestant Church. It is one of the oldest and most distinctive buildings in the Old Town. The projecting wooden gables and galleries which overlook the street were once a common feature of Edinburgh's townscape, a means not only of increasing floor space, but also of enabling residents to perambulate and take the air without having to descend to the frequently filthy streets below.

By the middle of the 18th century the Old Town, despite its royal and romantic associations with Scottish history, presented visitors with scenes of spectacular squalor, inducing the city's wealth and influence to move to the fashionable Georgian New Town. Proposals in 1752 to build the New Town on a plateau north of the Castle dismissed the steep, narrow wynds and closes (lanes and alleys) of the medieval city as 'so many avoidable nuisances' and noted that its tenements were 'more crowded than in any other town in Europe'.

These conditions persisted throughout the 19th century. Robert Louis Stevenson vividly described the Old Town as a 'black labyrinth' populated by '... skulking jailbirds, unkempt, barefoot children ... robust women in tartan shawls ... shrewd Scottish workmen ... a few supervising constables and a dismal sprinkling of mutineers and broken men from higher ranks of society ...' The Old Town had become a romantic slum.

The John Knox House was actually condemned as a 'dangerous ruin' but was saved from demolition because of its association with the famous reformer. From 1867 onwards attempts were made to improve conditions and rebuild the area. The tenement by the traffic lights on the right of the picture was one of the first to be put up during the Victorian improvement scheme. By 1905 two thirds of the old buildings in the Old Town had been demolished. Fortunately, the new Victorian buildings, with their Scottish baronial façades and crow-stepped gables, seem to have snuggled sympathetically into the existing townscape to the extent that they appear older than they really are. The same cannot be said for some additions built in the 1960s.

The legacy of earlier neglect can still be seen in occasional gap sites and run-down buildings but such is the historical importance of the Old Town that serious and sympathetic attempts are being made to conserve the area's traditional appearance while providing the amenities required by residents and visitors alike.

The earliest recorded settlement in Edinburgh was a fort on Castle Rock in the 6th century during which time the site was constantly fought over by rival tribal bands. Castle Rock is an extinct volcanic outcrop, precipitous on three sides but with a long slope to the east formed by Ice Age glaciers. It is a natural defensive position and has been of strategic importance throughout Scottish history.

By the 12th century a small town had grown under the protective gaze of the Castle and by the mid-15th century, despite the hiccups of frequent wars with England, the town, with its adjacent port at Leith, had become the 'principal burgh of Scotland'.

Left: *Romantic and floodlit in the gloaming. Seen at twilight, Edinburgh Castle sprawls on its summit above the National Gallery.*
Top: *Firing the One O'Clock Gun, a daily ritual and a popular spectacle for visitors. The soldier firing the gun has a stopwatch in his left hand, a necessary accessory as the clock behind him appears two minutes slow. The gun, a 25-pounder* of World War II vintage, makes a thunderous bang which can be heard across the city. The shell, no doubt to the relief of the people of Leith at whom it is aimed, is always a blank. The last time the Castle's guns fired in anger was in 1745 when the garrison briefly bombarded Holyrood Palace which had been occupied by Bonnie Prince Charlie.*
Above: *The Castle still retains a military presence.*

Edinburgh Castle has a rambling collection of old buildings whose silhouette looks as if it was cut by the Ice Age glaciers which scraped the rock clean. As you walk up the winding, cobbled pathways to its highest point (inside the Scottish National War Memorial) you can enter many places of interest. Notable things to see in the Castle include St Margaret's Chapel, the Great Hall, the French Prisons, Mons Meg (an elephantine 15th-century Flemish cannon), the Royal Palace (where the Scottish Crown is displayed), the room where Mary, Queen of Scots gave birth to James VI, the Scottish United Services Museum, the Royal Scots Regimental Museum and Scotland's impressive but melancholy Valhalla, the Scottish National War Memorial.

Left and far right: Two details from the many stained-glass windows depicting scenes from the two world wars and commemorating the Scottish soldiers who were killed in these and other 20th-century conflicts. The picture on the left shows soldiers at a railway station preparing to leave for the trenches of the Western Front during the First World War. The window reproduced on the right shows a similarly evocative scene as a battalion from a Scottish regiment boards a troopship for some distant foreign battlefield.

Right: Two contemporary Scottish soldiers in full regalia. They belong to the Argyll and Sutherland Highlanders and were photographed in a street near Murrayfield where their pipe band had been playing at a rugby international.

Top right: Baronial splendour in the Great Hall at Edinburgh Castle. Built by James IV in the early 16th century, it was restored by some over-enthusiastic Victorians who gave it what now seems the Hollywood touch of Citizen Kane's Xanadu. The hall retains its magnificent timber hammer-beam roof, a contemporary of which also survives in Scotland's old Parliament building by St Giles in the Royal Mile. Beneath the Great Hall are the gloomy vaults known as the French Prisons where prisoners-of-war were incarcerated during the Napoleonic Wars.

Considering their varied tribal and racial population – a *mélange* of Picts, Scots, Celtic Britons, Angles, Vikings, Flemish and Norman French – it's not surprising that the Scots are such a resourceful and inventive people or that their history is often documented as one turbulent episode after another. Scotland's history is a complex saga of periodic wars. When they weren't fighting amongst themselves, the Scots were fighting the English who viewed the country as an unstable northern neighbour susceptible to anti-English continental influence. Certainly Scotland's strong cultural and commercial connections with the Continent by-passed England. Indeed, the country's only enduring alliance was the 'Auld Alliance' with France which lasted from the late 13th until the late 16th century. This alliance, with its potential to frustrate their ambitions in Europe, exasperated the English and it opened a colourful, if violent, period in Scotland's history – the Wars of Independence.

During this time the English sent armies north to subdue Scotland and subjugate her people. These regular invasions by the 'Auld Enemy' were a major pre-occupation in Edinburgh's affairs. The city was vulnerably close to the Anglo/Scottish border and it changed hands many times.

Edward I of England, the 'Hammer of the

Scots', looted the Castle in 1296. The Earl of Moray, nephew of King Robert the Bruce who routed an English army at the Battle of Bannockburn near Stirling in 1314, re-captured the Castle in an audacious night

attack. With a small band of men he scaled the Castle's rocky defences, like stealthy pirates in a rowing boat swiftly capturing a Spanish galleon on a dark ocean. He then destroyed the citadel to deny its future use to the English, sparing only the 12th century

St Margaret's Chapel.

In 1322 Edward II's army sacked Holyrood Abbey, followed by Edward III in 1335 who rebuilt the Castle as an English fortress. But six years later it was re-captured and

demolished again. In 1385 and 1400 the English besieged the Castle and plundered the town in 1544 after a daring amphibious landing at Leith. Miraculously, St Margaret's Chapel survived these two centuries of conflict and it remains today the oldest

building on the site.

The chapel is named after Queen Margaret of Scotland, a Saxon princess who had been brought up by her family in exile in Hungary. About 1069 she married Malcolm III of Scotland who had come to the throne following the death of Macbeth, who had killed his father, King Duncan. Margaret died in 1093 after hearing news that her husband and eldest son had been killed in battle during a military incursion into England.

Queen Margaret was, by repute, a popular and benevolent queen and was canonised after her death. During her husband's rule she was able to bring a civilising and reforming influence to Scottish social and spiritual life and a degree of European sophistication to the Scottish court. Despite her influential position and her royal wealth, she apparently lived an ascetic life which seems testified to in the spartan interior of her chapel.

An interior of exquisite purity. St Margaret's Chapel showing the chancel arch built by David I in memory of his mother and stained-glass windows commemorating Queen Margaret and William Wallace, Scottish hero of the Wars of Independence. Every tourist or pilgrim who enters this beautiful, silent room cannot but be transfixed by its eloquent emptiness.

After a long climb from Princes Street or Holyrood, the visitor to Edinburgh Castle is rewarded with a superb view, often animated by clouds scudding across the city below. Approaching the Castle on foot also physically demonstrates the past military importance of its almost unassailable position in a way that arriving by air-conditioned coach can never do. Walking, which is the best way to explore central Edinburgh, allows you to make spontaneous detours in the maze of wynds and closes of the Old Town as you steadily ascend to Castle Rock. The views from the battlements are exhilarating, particularly east down the Royal Mile from the Half Moon Battery and north across the New Town from the Argyle Battery. The Half Moon and Argyle batteries are two of the many additions to the Castle's fortifications built over the years. The Argyle Battery dates from the 1730s and was built by General Wade, the renowned military engineer.

Far left: *Edinburgh Castle rears up above the traffic in Market Street.*
Left: *Chimneypots, spires and turrets tumble down the Royal Mile from the Castle's Half Moon Battery. In descending order are the black Gothic pinnacles of Tolbooth St John's Church, the turreted Outlook Tower (which has a camera obscura also giving a view of the city), the crowned tower of St Giles and the steeple of the Tron Kirk. The John Knox House and the flagpole and turrets of Holyrood Palace can just be seen on the extreme left of the picture.*

The highest viewpoint over Edinburgh is obtained from the summit of Arthur's Seat, an 800-foot high volcano (extinct!) in Holyrood Park within a stone's throw, well, almost, of the city centre. From here you get a 360-degree panorama and on a good day you can see the distant peaks of the Highlands and oil rigs out in the North Sea. The climb is well worth the effort but if you do it in mid-winter dress like an Eskimo.

Above: *Arthur's Seat, Edinburgh's Everest, with would-be mountaineers on the icy summit.*

Left: *The Victorian North British Hotel seen from the slopes of Arthur's Seat. Once viewed as a pompous intruder, it has matured to become an indispensible feature of the Edinburgh townscape. In the foreground are the chimneypots of the Old Town and North Bridge leaping out from the canyon between the NB Hotel and the Post Office building. Behind the hotel clock tower, perched on his Doric column above the banks in St Andrew Square, is the figure of Henry Dundas, 1st Viscount Melville, a powerful 18th-century Scottish politician. In the background, beyond the playing fields of Inverleith and a warship steaming up the River Forth to the Royal Navy base at Rosyth, are the rolling, snow-covered Ochil Hills.*

Edinburgh Castle seen from Arthur's Seat as late afternoon sunlight sends long shadows across the old city. The edge of the Salisbury Crags, an escarpment on the western slope of Arthur's Seat can be seen in the foreground. Flagstones once quarried from the Salisbury Crags were used to pave some Edinburgh streets and for a time were exported to London until the practice was stopped to preserve the picturesque quality of the area.

Overlooked by the Salisbury Crags is the dome of Edinburgh University's Old College. Also in the picture are the Castle Esplanade where the Military Tattoo is held every year, the glazed roofs of the Royal Scottish Museum, the ornamented pyramid roof on the Central Library, Tolbooth St John's Church and in the background, the dome of West Register House and the twin turrets of Daniel Stewart's and Melville College.

21

Above: *Canyon-like tenement façades in the Canongate, looking towards the Tron Kirk. The tradition of Scottish tenement building, which reached its apogee in the noble vistas of 19th-century Glasgow, began here in Edinburgh's Old Town. Within the walls of the 17th-century city there was nowhere to build but up.*

Top right: *Enamelled street signs and cast-iron railings.*
Centre: *At the lower end of Canongate sunset shadows creep up 'the mile of memories'.*
Right: *The mainly Victorian tenements in Ramsay Gardens. Their architectural style, a gallimaufry of balconies, crow-steps and gables, takes its cue from traditional 17th-century buildings in the Old Town.*
Far right: *The attractive gables of Huntly House in the Canongate. Inside what were once three townhouses converted to one in 1570 is an absorbing museum* *of local history which wanders over several floors. Until 1636 the Canongate was a separate burgh beyond the city walls, an exclusive suburb inhabited by wealthy merchants and aristocrats. A combination of fresh spring water and tax exemption also made it a good location for the breweries which were built incongruously among the salubrious townhouses close to Holyrood Palace.*

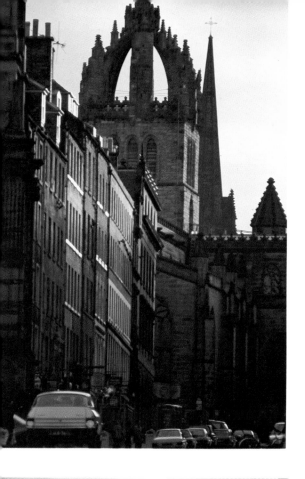

Left: *Catching the last rays of the sun, the spiky spire of St Giles dominates the tenements in the High Street. The High Kirk of St Giles is on the site of Edinburgh's original parish church dating from about the 12th century. The present building largely dates from the 15th century although the four central pillars are probably of 12th-century origin. Most of the exterior stonework and interior stained-glass is Victorian and the Thistle Chapel, designed by Sir Robert Lorimer (who was also responsible for the Scottish National War Memorial), was completed in 1911.*

Although the seat of the Reformation in Scotland (John Knox was the kirk's first Protestant minister), St Giles has since acquired an unusually elaborate interior for a Protestant church. One feels that if Knox returned today he would not wholly approve of the assorted statuary, including a memorial to the Marquis of Montrose, Scotland's much admired Royalist soldier who was brutally executed at the Mercat Cross outside the kirk in 1650, or the decoration in the Thistle Chapel which is almost Italian in its ostentation. And what would he make of the two carved angels who play the bagpipes there?

Remove the cars, traffic lights and television aerials and the Royal Mile could still be the medieval mile of narrow alleys, mysterious courtyards and chaotic streetlife. It is a mile of memories – of merchants concluding business deals in the open air at the Mercat Cross, tradesmen and hawkers peddling their wares from shambolic street stalls around St Giles and of black-hearted medieval hoodlums lurking in dark closes.

This is where the Scots/French cry of *gardyloo* warned pedestrians of slops descending to the streets from tenement windows eight or ten stories up, where, in the 18th century, inebriated judges would hold court sustained by claret and port, and where poets Robert Fergusson and Rabbie Burns and his coterie caroused the nights away. Edinburgh was a wild town where noblemen, ambassadors, churchmen and lawyers mingled with fishwives, beggars, poets and thieves.

This vigourously egalitarian social mix was diluted after the New Town was built and the gulf between wealth and poverty became a topographical feature. Stevenson remarked on the New Town's 'superimposition of one rank of society over another' where, by Victorian times, class-conscious planning had designated a 'hierarchy of parallel streets providing different classes of accommodation' as one local historian has observed. While the New Town's expansion created much fine architecture, it irreversibly changed the tenor of Edinburgh's urban life and engendered class attitudes and pretensions which would have rightly been ridiculed in the close-knit environment of the medieval town.

EDINBURGH CASTLE FROM GRASSMARKET. 28.

Although Edinburgh's Old Town has been rebuilt over the years many views remain resolutely unchanged. The Castle from the Grassmarket (top left) seen in the 1890s is as recognisable today as it would have been in the 1690s. The Grassmarket, however, is no longer the site of the bustling weekly market where travelling circuses entertained pedlars and passers-by alike. Nor does it witness riots, public executions or play stage to the activities of the murderous body-snatchers Burke and Hare, who supplied city physicians with bodies for medical research in the 19th century. Money could be made body-snatching in those days and such was the scale of this gruesome practice that special watchtowers were manned at night in Edinburgh churchyards to deter the grave-robbers. Burke and Hare, it seems, just couldn't get enough bodies so they turned to murdering beggars and whores, crimes for which Burke was eventually hanged in the Grassmarket having been implicated by Hare.

The John Knox House (bottom right) looks thoroughly dilapidated in this mid-19th-century photograph but it survives today. The Newhaven fishwives (bottom left) who used to sell their North Sea herring in the High Street have vanished along with their trade. The two Gordon Highlanders (far left) based in the Castle in 1846 are mirror images of Highlanders still to be seen today. (All three of these photographs are by the early Edinburgh photographers, Hill and Adamson.) The stunning 1969 aerial photograph (top right) showing 'Auld Reekie', its monuments petrified in a sea of fog, is nowadays a less familiar sight. The famous North Sea haar still shrouds the city from time to time but Edinburgh is becoming smoke-free and its nickname, coined by folk on the Fife coast who could tell it was dinner time by the amount of smoke issuing from Edinburgh's chimneypots, will soon be an affectionate memory.

The Palace of Holyroodhouse was originally built as an enlargement of the Abbey guest house by James IV who began the work in 1501. The twin-turreted north-west tower, completed in 1532, is all that remains of this original design. The Palace was almost entirely rebuilt by Charles II to whom it owes much of its appearance today. During the 18th and 19th centuries the Palace was infrequently used although it had a brief return to former sparkle when Bonnie Prince Charlie held court during the 1745 rebellion.

Edinburgh's status as a centre of the Stuart court ended one night in March 1603 when an exhausted, mud-bespattered nobleman arrived at the gates of Holyrood having ridden the 400 miles from London in three days to inform James VI that Elizabeth I was dead and that he was to be the next King of England. After the Union of the Crowns, English affairs dominated court life, a situation exacerbated in 1707 by the Union of the Parliaments from which Scotland, emotionally and arguably in other ways, has never recovered. Stevenson, no doubt in a fit of national pique, declared that Holyrood had become '... no more than a show for tourists and a museum of old furniture'.

Well, it's still a 'show for tourists and a museum of old furniture' although since late-Victorian days it has enjoyed more regular royal patronage and restoration. Visitors are given discreet and carefully organised tours of its royal apartments. The largely 17th-century interiors, characterised by lavish Louis XIV wood and plasterwork decoration, are certainly worth seeing. There's also an amazing picture gallery containing 111 portraits of Scottish monarchs painted by a Dutch artist, Jacob de Witt.

Did de Witt have his wits about him when he signed the contract for the work in 1684? He undertook to 'produce the said paintings within two years' (a rate of one and a wee bit a week) and 'to make them like unto the originals' (old portraits with which he was supplied). Well, he finished the pictures in time, presumably to royal satisfaction, although not to Sir Walter Scott's, who observed that many of the kings portrayed

'... if they ever flourished at all, lived several hundred years before the invention of painting in oils'. De Witt, despite his tedious task, had some imagination after all. At least 30 of his kings never existed.

Holyrood was also witness to many events in the chequered career of Scotland's sad Catholic queen, Mary, Queen of Scots. It was the setting for several intense but finally inconclusive meetings between Mary and John Knox which followed her arrival from France in 1561 when she had undermined her initial popularity by attending mass in her private chapel despite a Protestant mob outside and Knox's protests from the pulpit of St Giles.

In 1566, Mary's Italian secretary, David Rizzio, who was rumoured to be her paramour and thought to be influencing her politics, was stabbed to death by her jealous husband Darnley and his confederates. The intrigue deepened when Darnley was blown up by gunpowder the following year at Kirk o' Field (on a site now occupied by Edinburgh University's Old College). Mary then married the Earl of Bothwell who was suspected of the revengeful crime. She was forced to abdicate, imprisoned, fled into exile in England and was eventually executed on the orders of her cousin, Elizabeth I of England.

Left: *Arthur's Seat and the turreted roofline of Holyrood Palace with the jumble of houses at the bottom of the Royal Mile aglow in a long, low burst of winter sunlight. In the foreground is New Calton Graveyard on the south slope of Calton Hill.*

Above: *Ornamental sign on the wall of Lady Stair's House. Edinburgh's streets, particularly in the Old Town, display a wide range of picturesque, decorative signwork.*

Top: *'Beware the eleventh step' evokes the medieval Edinburgh of skulduggery and mischief and cautious visitors to Lady Stair's House.*

Above: *Golden hawk above the entrance to Gladstone's Land. The owner of the building, one Thomas Gledstanes (Hawkstones), a 17th-century cloth merchant, adopted the hawk as a play on his surname.*

Top: *The Painted Chamber inside Gladstone's Land. An interesting contrast to Gladstone's Land is the Georgian House in Charlotte Square (also owned by the National Trust for Scotland).*

Right: *Sir Walter Scott posthumously advertises fountain pens on an enamelled tin sign in Blair Street.*

A number of old buildings on the Royal Mile, like Huntly House and the John Knox House, now function as museums. The Canongate Tolbooth, once the Canongate municipal building, has been converted into a museum and the nearby Acheson House has become a craft centre. The Netherbow Arts Centre mounts a variety of exhibitions in a new building designed to look old.

Gladstone's Land in the Lawnmarket is particularly interesting. At first a smaller building, it was extended by its new owner, Thomas Gledstanes, who bought it in 1617. It is a typical *land* (tenement) of the early 17th-century. Rising six storeys above the street (some later tenements were ten or twelve storeys high) it is arcaded on the ground floor, a device which has been revived in some recent buildings in the Old Town. Gladstone's Land has been restored by the National Trust for Scotland, a restoration which revealed under years of plaster the building's most amazing feature, the Painted Chamber with its Scandinavian-inspired painted ceiling.

Lady Stair's House in a courtyard behind Gladstone's Land is also a museum – a museum of literary memorabilia relating to Robert Burns, Sir Walter Scott and Robert Louis Stevenson. Wandering through this house it's not difficult to imagine the days of the 18th and 19th centuries when Edinburgh was a cockpit of cultural fervour, when the city's howffs were meeting places for clubs whose members joined from all ranks of society – barbers, brewers, advocates and musicians, painters, printers, surgeons and shipowners.

Below: *Above the tartan, tweed and knitwear shops at street level, the John Knox House is now a museum of the famous man and the Scottish Reformation. An interesting feature of the building is the pantile roof, a reminder of Edinburgh's traditional trade with the Low Countries and Scandinavia. The tiles were landed at Leith having been used as ballast on sailing ships returning to Scotland.*

Scotland's much fought-for independence was voted away by 110 votes to 69 by the Scottish Parliament in favour of the Union with the English Parliament which took place in 1707. The country was virtually bankrupt following the failure of an ambitious expedition to colonise part of what is now Panama – the 'Darien disaster' – a failure brought about as much by paranoid opposition from English vested interests as by the Spanish who were already colonists in the area. The expedition which left Leith in 1698 was a national calamity. In addition to the opposition described above, the Scots found the area a fever-ridden swamp and 'New Edinburgh', as their settlement was called, was abandoned with great loss of life.

There was considerable argument about the Union at the time – and riots in Edinburgh and Glasgow. Glasgow, however, did gain from the Union of Parliaments. Its enterprising merchants claimed access to English overseas possessions and their city rose to wealth and influence on the tobacco trade with the colonies in America. By the end of the 19th century, Glasgow was the 'industrial, commercial and artistic capital of Scotland', the 'second city of the greatest empire the world has known'. It still claims the former distinction and the droll rivalry which exists between the two cities can be traced to Glasgow's rise after the Union. Edinburgh had lost its royalty in 1603, its Parliament in 1707 and with these two institutions went much of the city's influence. Meanwhile, 45 miles to the west, Edinburgh's temporarily wounded establishment saw a parvenu Glasgow on the make.

Some Scottish institutions did retain their autonomy after the Union of Parliaments. The Church of Scotland guarded its hard-won freedoms and Scotland's education, legal and to a lesser extent, banking systems remain today separate from those south of the Border. While the banks and financial institutions in Edinburgh have moved to the New Town, a reflection of their expansion during the 19th century, the law, the Church,

and local government are still based in the heart of the Old Town.

Opposite page: *The opulent Upper Hall in the Signet Library (1815) in Parliament Square, was described by George IV in 1822 as the most beautiful room he had ever seen, a response perhaps conditioned by the shabby state of Holyrood Palace at the time where he had refused to stay while on his visit to Edinburgh. Nevertheless, the Upper Hall is impressive and is beautifully maintained by the Society of Writers to Her Majesty's Signet (an historic organisation of eminent Scottish lawyers founded in 1594). The Signet Library remains as much a manifestation of Scotland's legal independence as court procedure. Only the Scots could invent the sternly suspicious verdict 'Not Proven' with its overtones of disapproval and future social stigma for the accused.*

Above: *The former Royal High School (1829) by Thomas Hamilton is a building of international stature, the 'noblest monument to the Scottish Greek Revival'. Sited on the side of Calton Hill below the National and Nelson Monuments, it gives credence to Edinburgh's 19th-century soubriquet the 'Athens of the North'. During the resurgent nationalism of the 1970s when Edinburgh was again at the centre of political debate, the building was converted to become the proposed Scottish National Assembly, but plans were aborted by a tendentious government reaction which ignored a positive referendum result. On the far left skyline of the picture St Andrew's House, completed in 1939 for the Scottish Office of the British Government, can just be seen. It has some nice Art Deco details fashionable at the time, but there's nothing Hollywood about the building. It's the sort of edifice which European dictators had a taste for at the time.*

Left: *Scottish contradictions juxtaposed on the skyline of the Old Town. The black spire of Tolbooth St John's Church looms like a reproachful conscience above the dome of the Bank of Scotland. Such symbolism would have been clearly understood by Edinburgh's prosperous God-fearing merchants of the 18th and 19th centuries. They founded schools, funded libraries, religious and other charitable works, a tradition which goes back to 1624 when George Heriot, James VI's goldsmith, left his fortune to the city to endow a 'hospital' for orphans (now a school). Indeed, Edinburgh's Merchant Company, founded in 1681 by a royal charter from Charles II to protect its members' trading rights, embarked on a programme of charitable and educational work in the city which it continues today.*

Below: *The Merchant Company's coat of arms above their Hanover Street doorway.*

Left: *Palatial financial façades in St Andrew Square. Edinburgh's banks proclaimed their wealth and stability in sumptuous stonework and interior decoration.*

Right: *Corinthian columns and a sculptural tableau adorn the portico of the Royal Bank of Scotland's George Street building, built in 1847 and based on a design by William Playfair. Commenting on its appearance and expense the 'Scotsman' observed approvingly '. . . as our merchants are princes, why should they not have palaces?'*
Far right: *The building's banking hall embellished with plasterwork, pilasters and a delicately-tiled floor overhung by a glazed, stained-glass dome supported on marble columns. Interestingly, a facsimile exists in Canada. Emigré Scots financiers looking for a worthy precedent for their planned Bank of Montreal head office copied the George Street building.*

Bottom right: *'Sumptuous stonework' on the Bank of Scotland in St Andrew Square. This extravagant 1852 elevation by David Bryce was clearly meant to impress when it flamboyantly elbowed its way into the elegant monotony of Edinburgh's Georgian New Town. The figures balanced on top of the façade represent Agriculture, Science, Art, Industry, Commerce and Navigtion.*

Below: *The astonishing starlit iron dome in the Royal Bank of Scotland's banking hall in St Andrew Square. It looks like a scene from the Arabian Nights.*

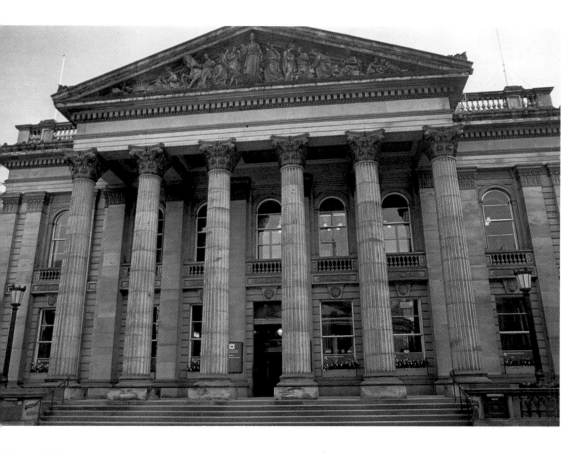

Edinburgh, in terms of funds moved, is said to be the second most important financial centre in Europe, after the City of London. Judging from the palatial banking headquarters and insurance buildings in and around St Andrew Square this claim is probably true. If Glasgow built the steamships and locomotives to run the 'Scottish Empire' then Edinburgh banking, in part, financed it. Indeed, the industrial and mercantile wealth of Victorian Scotland is personified as much in the financial façades of St Andrew Square as it is in the commercial buildings of Glasgow's 19th-century city centre. The British Empire provided many openings for Scots quick to seize their opportunities. It certainly exploited their military traditions and encouraged massive emigration but it also prompted economic development at home and enabled companies and individuals to amass huge fortunes, which promptly found their way into Edinburgh's capacious bank vaults.

Princes Street, Edinburgh's main thoroughfare, not only faces the spectacular panorama of the Castle and the Royal Mile on its unbuilt south side but also has two memorable urban vistas.

Above: *The view east past the North British Hotel to the 'medley of monuments' on Calton Hill, showing the columns of the National Monument of the Napoleonic Wars, begun in 1826 but never completed, and to their right Nelson's Monument of 1816, designed appropriately in the shape of an upturned*

telescope. The National Monument was supposed to look like the Parthenon but the money ran out after only 12 of the 46 columns had been erected. Obviously there wasn't a market at the time for 12 slightly used Doric columns so they were left there to become a picturesque hilltop folly.

While Edinburgh in the summertime becomes a lively, cosmopolitan, festival and tourist city, under leaden winter skies it assumes a brooding dignity. Stevenson thought the weather 'raw and boisterous'

in winter and it can certainly be damp and dreich. But winter has its moments. The weather plays unpredictable atmospheric tricks. Hazy sunlight silhouettes monuments with an enigmatic, etherial presence. Soft snowfalls and frosty days with crystal light as clear as the famous Edinburgh glassware hold the city in a spellbound hush. Frequently, Siberian winds sweep the broad streets of the New Town and whistle down the alleys of the Old. People scurry for shelter, until, suddenly, the wind will stop. And in the short, silent period before the streets fill again, Stevenson's 'ancient and famous Metropolis of the North' becomes a romantic ghost town.

Above: *Victorian spires and gables silhouetted in late afternoon winter sunlight at the west end of Princes Street. The picture shows Queen Victoria on top of the Royal Scottish Academy's portico, the gable of the Caledonian Hotel, St John's Church, the Venetian-style campanile of St George's West Church and the triple spires of St Mary's Cathedral, an immobile backdrop for rush hour traffic.*

Above: *An old postcard view of Princes Street about 1885. The familiar monuments remain but many of the buildings on the right have been demolished. In the left foreground are the gardens on the roof of the old cast-iron Waverley Market, once used for exhibitions, carnivals and flower shows, but now replaced by a shopping centre.*

Left: *The west end of Princes Street snowbound at the turn of the century. Cable cars which ran along the street before plunging San Francisco style down Frederick, Hanover or Leith Streets have vanished along with the ornate cast-iron clock. Otherwise the scene is similar today. The churches are St John's and, in the middle-distance, St Cuthbert's steeple.*

Frozen in these old photographs, Princes Street seems to have changed little since the 19th century. Designed as part of the New Town, it was originally a residential street offering what contemporary estate agents' hyperbole might have described (accurately) as 'exceptional views of the Castle'.

As Edinburgh grew in the 19th century, Princes Street's position, on the edge of the New Town but in sight of the medieval city, caused it to become the natural centre of the developing metropolis. It was connected to the Old Town by two bridges and the Mound (a huge earthwork made from excavations in the New Town) and soon became Edinburgh's principal shopping street.

Two centuries of change have seen most of its original Georgian buildings replaced but such is the strength of its natural setting, it seems to have hardly changed at all. It even survived a bold but potentially disastrous 1960s scheme to rebuilt the street with what could have been a monotonous line of concrete blocks. Today, while no longer Georgian, it is not completely modern either. It's a hotch-potch of mainly Victorian and modern architectural styles, not all distinguished, but on balance, generally pleasing.

Top right: *Princes Street about 1875 in another postcard view. The top-hatted gentlemen and the horse and carriage add a period touch to the scene. Conspicuous by its absence is the North British Railway Company's hotel which was built in the 1890s.*

Right: *A spectacular tram jam in Princes Street about 1950 taken by an enterprising 'Scotsman' photographer who scrambled up the Scott Monument for the view. The trams, originally horsedrawn, began running from Leith to Edinburgh in 1871. Cable cars were introduced on the more precipitous routes in 1888 and the whole system was electrified in 1923. Hold-ups like the one shown, although a rare occurence, gave these otherwise sedate, reliable and economic vehicles a bad name and the trams were, regrettably, replaced by buses in 1956.*

PRINCES STREET FROM NATIONAL GALLERY EDINBURGH. 465. J.V.

Left: *Princes Street at night seen from Waterloo Place. In the distance, solemn spires frown on the glittering boulevard.*

Above right: *The floodlit façade of the fin-de-siècle Caledonian Hotel, built for the Caledonian Railway Company. The 19th-century railway barons had firm views on architecture. 'Any style as long as it's impressive' they would say to their willing architects. For the Caledonian Hotel, an unlikely but likable blend of Dutch Baroque and French Second Empire was chosen, with a bit of Renaissance detail added for good measure. An interesting comparison can be seen nearby in Lothian Road opposite the Usher Hall. The Edinburgh Sheraton is a modern hotel which has unobtrusively appeared in the city townscape. Its stone-clad, gabled façade and glistening interior re-interprets the Edwardian luxury evident in the Caledonian.*

Above: *The entrance to the Edinburgh Sheraton.*

Princes Street at night, especially once a week when the shops and department stores open late, gives Edinburgh an ersatz metropolitan feel. It's not exactly Broadway, but why should it be? Edinburgh is not a large city and it has not been tarnished by the rat-race. For all its financial wealth, there is no downtown business district of glass tower blocks and there are no motorways. Business is conducted in the elegant sobriety of converted Georgian townhouses and in ornate Victorian banking halls and boardrooms. Edinburgh with its over-powering and civilising sense of history seems to have resisted the urban excesses of the 20th century, much as Florence or Vienna have done.

Below: *Sunset along Princes Street seen from Waterloo Place framed by the North British Hotel (left) and Register House.*

A winter evening in Edinburgh. Wet streets with commuters making their way to Waverley Station, hundreds of lights like Christmas trees on a canyon wall twinkle in the Old Town, cups tinkle as the coffee houses and tea rooms close, fur coats and other fashions congregate at theatres and concert halls, clans gather in chandeliered function rooms and in the steamed-up bars, local bureaucrats, bankers, lawyers and labourers linger over their whiskies and Younger's beer.

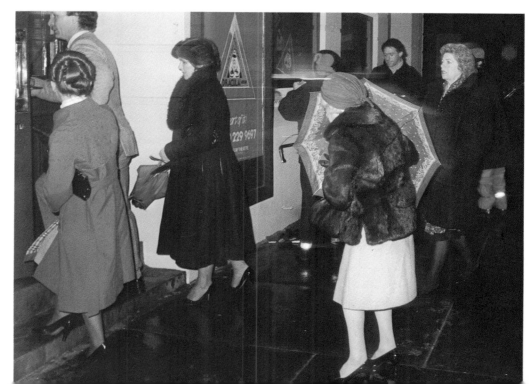

Edinburgh's literary heritage is perpetuated not only in the city's many bookshops and publishing houses but also in its main railway station, named in the 1840s after the Sir Walter Scott novel. There's no mistaking Waverley Station with its sprawling glass canopy covering semi-subterranean platforms and its dominant North British Hotel.

Most railway lines into cities in the 19th century tended to be above ground, high on viaducts and brick arches, leading to glorious temples of steam. Waverley is at basement level. It seems designed to reveal nothing of the city until, that is, the exhausted arriving passenger walks up the long ramp to ground level to be stunned by the famous view which greets him.

Left: *Patterns of Victorian iron and glass glimpsed from the entrance ramp of Waverley station.*

Right: *The National Gallery of Scotland must be the only art gallery in the world with three railway tunnels running directly underneath.*

Below: *Belching steam locomotives once added to Edinburgh's smoky atmosphere. Today 'Auld Reekie' is no more but colourfully-painted coal lorries still deliver to areas not yet affected by smokeless zones.*

Left: *In the 1890s Waverley was described as 'a scene of confusion' with 'bewildered crowds of tourists' and railway officials 'lost in subtle thought' no doubt wondering why so many trains were late – not a description likely to appeal to British Rail. The reason for the delays – trains queued up to use the platforms – was that the completion of the Forth Railway Bridge had caused a huge increase in traffic and Waverley had to be rebuilt around this time.*

THE FORTH BRIDGE.
INCHCARVIE FROM THE WIND GAUGES.
APRIL 6 1888. N.º 251.

Edinburgh is not an industrial city but on the horizon (you can see it from the Castle) or 15 minutes by train from Waverley is one of *the* monuments of the Industrial Revolution – the Forth Railway Bridge. Like Edinburgh's other famous sights, it has appeared on countless postcards and oatcake tins. It was even the location for a dramatic escape from a train in Hitchcock's film of the *Thirty Nine Steps.*

The Bridge is over 1½ miles long and it took an army of 4000 men 7 years to build between 1883 and 1890. The workforce was mainly Scottish but it also included Irish, Welsh, English, French, Belgians, Germans, Italians and Austrians – many in specialist capacities. A French contractor who had experience of similar work on the Danube and the Suez Canal was employed to sink the underwater foundations for chief engineers John Fowler (English) and Benjamin Baker, a Welshman. The main contractor was the Glasgow firm of William Arrol (this famous company also worked on the adjacent Forth Road Bridge completed in 1964). All three men were knighted for their contribution to the building of the railway bridge.

Even today, although with only one hundredth of the 1880s workforce, it takes about 4 years to complete a full maintenance programme including re-painting the 54,000 tons of steelwork, by which time, as legend has it, they start all over again. The red paint, made to a special recipe, is still supplied by the Edinburgh firm which developed it 100 years ago.

Above: *The Forth Railway Bridge is used by about 200 trains every 24 hours, including expresses from Dundee and Aberdeen to Edinburgh and London.*

Left: *The heroic era of Victorian engineering. The Forth Railway Bridge under construction in 1888. The picture shows the bridge taking shape like a giant meccano set and gives some idea of the colossal scale of construction.*

Below: *Edinburgh's own 'Golden Gates', the Forth Road and Rail Bridges spanning the estuary between South and North Queensferry.*

Princes Street Gardens were laid out in the early 19th century for the benefit of the wealthy residents of the New Town – a place where 'genteel folk might walk at all times without risk of meeting improper persons'. A notice warned 'that any person entering these gardens without a legal right will be prosecuted'. This was no doubt to deter 'improper persons' from the tenements of the Old Town, an example of the 'ostentatious social inequality' of the time to which Stevenson referred.

Stevenson lampooned the 'conscious moral rectitude' of these New Town citizens who 'kept ledgers and attended church'. His criticism was not appreciated and it is perhaps not surprising that while Princes Street Gardens boast a monolithic monument to Sir Walter Scott, who largely

confined his writings to romanticising Scottish history, there is to date not one

Above and below: The Ross Fountain in West Princes Street Gardens.

Right: Princes Street Gardens and the Scott Monument. On the left, the hubbub of Princes Street. On the right, the gardens provide an escape to sylvan tranquillity. Once privately owned, they were opened to the public in 1876.

public monument in the whole of Edinburgh to Stevenson.

Edinburgh's stiff-necked morality was given further voice in 1869 when the Ross Fountain, shipped from France by a city gunsmith, was unveiled. At first glance it seems a decorously florid piece of Victorian cast-iron, decorated with nymphs, mermaids and Grecian ladies. Until you look at the top, that is. One of the nymphs bares a glorious golden bum for all to see. A local preacher saw it and pronounced the fountain 'grossly indecent and disgusting'. What would he have thought of the strippers who perform at lunchtimes in some city bars? Even on Sundays. I asked some if I could photograph them too. But they were all more bashful than the Victorian beauty on top of the Ross Fountain.

'I am sorry to report the Scott Monument a failure. It is like the spire of a church taken off and stuck in the ground.' Charles Dickens.

'It is . . . the central and supreme object in the architecture of our present Edinburgh . . . the finest which has yet been raised anywhere on earth to the memory of a man of letters.' 'The Scotsman'.

The Scott Monument aroused strong feelings in the 19th century, not always favourable. Some critics weren't surprised to discover that the designer, George Meikle Kemp, was completely self-taught. But public opinion supported his inspired competition design and construction began in 1840.

The monument is an incredible 200 foot high Gothic fantasy, an architectural brainstorm of buttresses, pillars, pinnacles, arches and 64 stone statues (mainly characters from Scott's novels) with Scott himself, carved in Carrara marble, at its base. In a sense the building is also a memorial to its designer who fell into a canal and drowned before it was completed – one way of escaping the prejudice which had branded him 'an obscure man' and opposed his competition entry. Yet his building is remembered by tourists long after others have been forgotten.

Above: *The ebullient Victorian baroque façade of Jenners department store, built in 1895 and one of the few traditional stores left in Princes Street, attempts to out-decorate the Scott Monument across the street.*

Left: *The Scott Monument seen from St Andrew Square on a silent Edinburgh Sunday morning.*

Below: *A literary epigram on a tin sign outside the Waverley and Cameron Pen Company in Blair Street.*

Left: *The 'hoots mon' syndrome or a genuine Scottish identity? Tartan ties in Princes Street.*
Above: *Tartan packaging is rarely sophisticated but can often be endearingly kitsch. The masthead of Edinburgh's morning newspaper, however, is a classic piece of graphic design.*
Far right: *Highland soldiers in stained glass evoke imperial battles of long ago, their tartan, while not the best camouflage, a proud symbol of regimental and national identity.*

Edinburgh, more than any other Scottish city, cultivates a veneer of specious Scottishness. It's tartan town. Princes Street and the Royal Mile are chock-a-block with shops selling Highland crafts, kilts, sporrans and bagpipes designed, you would think, to enable the customer whether he hails from Texas or Tokyo to return home and attend fancy-dress parties as a Highland chieftain. And if you have any ancestral connection with a Scottish clan—no matter how tenuous—there are shops in Edinburgh which will supply you with an appropriate tartan from the hundreds invented in Victorian times.

There are many more Scots and people of Scottish descent overseas—50 million according to a recent estimate—than the 5 million or so in Scotland. In summer time it seems the former are all in Edinburgh. Most are rightly proud of their Scottish connections, are happy to embrace the country's culture and they sustain Edinburgh's tourist trade as an established and economically important part of city life. Edinburgh as a tourist attraction certainly dates back to 1822 when George IV, encouraged by Sir Walter Scott, landed at the Port of Leith and paraded up to Holyrood Palace. A notable feature of this royal visit was the presence in the city of a large number of Highlanders dressed in full regalia who participated in the ceremonies. After the 1745 rebellion tartan had been outlawed in a ruthless attempt to demoralise, indeed eliminate, the Jacobites and the Highland clans which supported them and by 1822 the clans had been tamed, their communities de-populated during the Highland Clearances.

That anglophile Edinburgh was the stage for the rehabilitation of the Highlander during the visit of a king whose dynasty had persecuted the clans almost out of existence is one of the great ironies of Scottish history. The result of the 1822 celebrations was to legitimise a bowdlerised national culture, perpetuated all over Edinburgh today in the colourful, romantic but ultimately bogus infatuation with tartanry. If visitors have

difficulty seeing through all this Scotch mist it's just as hard for the Scots themselves. The line between pastiche of and pride in their origins is a tricky one to balance on—especially as pastiche is so profitable. Edinburgh exhibits both the excesses and the true expression of Scotland's cultural identity in the tartan shops of Princes Street and, for example, in the purity of St Margaret's Chapel.

Edinburgh is the seat of the Scottish establishment and since the Union of 1707 it has been traditionally anglophile. In 1787 when Robert Burns was being praised in the city for his poems in Scottish dialect a book was published in Edinburgh designed to 'correct (Scottish) improprieties in speech and writing'. This perhaps appealed to gentlemen 'who wished to improve their knowledge of the English toungue'—at the expense of their Scottish one—and who were of the opinion that an educated

Scotsman should communicate in English. All the same, the Edinburgh establishment's attachment to English mores did help Scotland become a force in European civilisation of the time. Indeed, Edinburgh in the late 18th century was 'one of the great cultural centres of Europe'—the hub of the Scottish Enlightenment.

While this was a time of considerable intellectual, scientific and artistic progress, it was at the expense of Scotland's traditionally strong trading and cultural links with the Baltic, the Low Countries and France which had developed independently of influence from south of the Border. These, and Scotland's historic struggle for independence, were consigned to antiquarian irrelevance. The decaying Old Town, glowering down on the New, visually symbolised the cultural condition of the time and when history was reappraised in 1822 it was cloaked in a tartan sham.

Scotland's tartan mythology is paraded and televised worldwide during the annual Edinburgh Military Tattoo, probably the most familiar aspect of the Edinburgh International Festival. The Festival, first held in 1947 as a gesture to help mend cultural wounds in Europe following the Second World War, has grown to become the foremost festival of its kind in the world. It has many imitators but none can rival the range of theatre, opera, dance, music, film, literature and visual arts which characterise the Edinburgh event – nor match its location in the centre of 'one of Europe's most beautiful cities'.

While the Festival, and especially the Tattoo, always have a Scottish element, it is essentially an international event of the highest quality. Indeed, the quest for excellence, by which the continuing reputation of the Festival is measured, has brought accusations of cultural élitism from some quarters which view it as an irrelevant, arty jamboree. Such parochial carping is not a new aspect of Scottish society and it perhaps owes its origin to the secretly envious, self-righteous Calvinism which once actually banned theatres in the city. In fact over half the ticket sales annually are to local people who, if they dream of stardom, can also join in on the unofficial Festival Fringe where anyone can perform.

Left: *The Edinburgh Military Tattoo, performed on summer evenings during the Festival in the artificial amphitheatre constructed annually on the Castle Esplanade.*

Left, top to bottom: *Signpost at Waverley Bridge, Festival Fringe posters and street performers in the Royal Mile.*

Edinburgh's entertainment is not confined to the three weeks at the end of August when the Festival is held. Throughout the year there are numerous events of a variety to be expected in any major city. Scottish Opera and the Scottish National Orchestra tour during the winter from Glasgow. The Scottish Chamber Orchestra and the Scottish Ensemble are resident in the city. City theatre companies like the Royal Lyceum and the Traverse enjoy a high reputation for both traditional and contemporary drama. The International Film Festival runs an innovative programme during the Festival proper and there is an annual folk festival held in early spring at Edinburgh University.

The city's art galleries and museums display rich and wide-ranging permanent collections and host an unceasing and stimulating flow of visiting exhibitions.

The pictures show Polish dancers at the Edinburgh Folk Festival, Victorian architectural details in the auditorium and foyer of the Royal Lyceum Theatre, built in 1883 and recently restored in appropriately gaudy style, Edinburgh's Polish Society dance band in national dress at the Folk Festival and cellos and a school chorus waiting to perform in the cavernous Edwardian interior of the Usher Hall.

The National Gallery of Scotland, the National Gallery of Modern Art, the National Portrait Gallery and the Royal Scottish Museum in Edinburgh, along with the Burrell Collection, Kelvingrove Museum and Art Gallery and the Hunterian Art Gallery in Glasgow, firmly place central Scotland on the itinerary of any serious European grand tour. Among the important paintings, for example, on display in Edinburgh's extensive collections are works by Degas, Dürer, Van Gogh, Goya, Pissarro, Poussin, Raphael, Rembrandt, Titian and Turner. The city's internationally renowned collections of fine art are complemented by the outstanding decorative art, ethnography, natural history, science and technology exhibits in the Royal Scottish Museum.

Opposite page: Paintings from the collection of the National Gallery of Scotland: Gauguin's 'Three Tahitians' (top), an appropriate picture for Edinburgh as Stevenson, like Gauguin, ended his career in the South Seas. 'The Rev Robert Walker skating on Duddingston Loch' by Sir Henry Raeburn (right), Scotland's most famous portrait painter. 'The Piazzetta, Venice' by Turner (left), one of 38 stunning watercolours from the Vaughan Bequest, exhibited only in low January light, a condition of the bequest to ensure their preservation.
Bottom right: No, not a Greek temple, but the south portico of the Royal Scottish Academy, like the adjacent National Gallery, designed by William Playfair.

Above: Roy Lichtenstein's 'In The Car' and Edinburgh's best-known tourists – lifesize fibreglass dummies who appear to have mistaken the city for Honolulu – arrest the attention in the Gallery of Modern Art in Belford Road.
Right: The entrance hall to the National Portrait Gallery and the National Museum of Antiquities, an elaborate Victorian building modelled on the Doge's Palace in Venice but lacking the original's pastel-coloured, arcaded elegance and the bravura of Glasgow's Victorian version (Templeton's Carpet Factory). The gallery has some redeeming features, notably its collections and the two-storey entrance hall which, with its frieze of characters from Scottish history, murals of the Battles of Bannockburn and Largs and arcaded gallery, has an agreeable architectural ambience.

The idyllic Royal Botanic Gardens, which moved to their present site at Inverleith in 1824, are a favourite spot for an outing. They have the bonus that in Edinburgh's chilly winter you can warm yourself up in the steamy sub-tropical interior of the Palm House. The first palm house was opened in 1834 but within 20 years some of the trees had burst through the roof, so a new palm house was built next door, an attractive sandstone, iron and glass building, completed in 1858. When the new palm house was opened a journalist was inspired to write that 'the tropical aspect . . . is heightened by the fact that the man in attendance upon visitors is a bona fide African', and added that 'a native of the sunny climes, where the palm trees grow, is better able to stand the high temperature of such a house than one of our own pale-faced race'. The African's comments are not recorded.

Left and above: *The 1858 iron and glass roofed Palm House in the Royal Botanic Gardens.*
Right: *Almost contemporary with the Botanic Garden's Palm House is the soaring cast-iron main hall in the Royal Scottish Museum in Chambers Street. Built in 1861, it was designed by Captain Francis Fowke, an army engineer, and it allows the multifarious exhibits to decorate the building rather than the other way round – as is the case in the more architecturally sententious museums which the Victorians had a tendency to build.*

Edinburgh Zoo, established in 1913 on the slopes of Corstorphine Hill, is hugely popular and has a reputation for breeding endangered species and a progressive policy of exhibiting its animals in as natural an environment as possible. Among the interesting facts which the zoo reveals about its animals is the food bill. The Siberian tiger gnaws its way through 40 pounds of meat a week and the sea lions seem to be keeping Edinburgh's numerous fishmongers in business – three of them consume 70 pounds of fish per day! Probably the most popular creatures on display are the penguins. Edinburgh has a worldwide reputation in zoological circles for breeding its penguins and the colony is the largest outside Antarctica.

Below: *Edinburgh Zoo and the penguins on parade.*

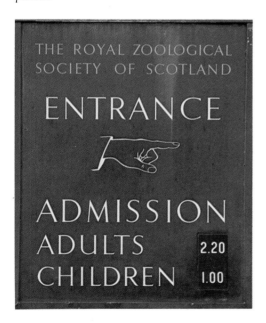

In Edinburgh you can play or watch virtually any sport you please. The city periodically hosts the Commonwealth Games at Meadowbank Stadium and the Royal Commonwealth Pool. It has in Hibernian and Heart of Midlothian (Hibs and Hearts) two traditionally competitive football teams – Edinburgh's version of Celtic and Rangers in Glasgow. One of the oldest golf courses in Scotland is at Leith Links and the city boasts the largest artificial ski slope in Britain. Rugby is one of the most popular sports in the city and the internationals are among its more colourful events. Every year at least three internationals are played at Murrayfield (the national stadium) – against France, England, Ireland, Wales or an overseas team.

The Welsh game is possibly the most festive, certainly off the pitch. Every second year, Edinburgh is invaded by Welsh hordes who, if they make it out of the bars in Rose Street, sing their way along Princes Street to the bewildered amusement of Saturday shoppers. At Murrayfield they're met by thousands of Scottish supporters (who've also extricated themselves from the Rose Street bars) waving yellow flags decorated with the Scottish lion and rugby honours. Scotland against Wales, France, Ireland, England and anybody else for that matter, is one great boozy binge. However, the 'demon drink' is banned inside the ground and crowd behaviour is generally good-natured. Of course, rugby supporters don't all drink. 'Well, maybe just a wee dram, medicinal of course, it's a cold day.'

Above and left: *The banners of the dragon and the lion. Welsh supporters on their way to Murrayfield – they appear to be holding the necessary liquid refreshment – and Scottish schoolboys inside the stadium.*

Right: *Motor-racing at Ingliston.*

The acres of Ingliston near the airport see not only regular motor-racing and the annual Royal Highland Show (Scotland's premier agricultural fair) but also are the location for what is said to be the largest outdoor market in Europe – Ingliston Sunday Market – held every weekend. Bus-loads of people come from all over the country to the market which manages to re-create someting of the medieval atmosphere of the markets once held in Edinburgh's Old Town. The place is full of stalls – mostly bargain basement – selling everything from gimcrack ornaments and tourist trifles to genuine antiques, cheap clothing, bamboo furniture and butcher meat. But don't be fooled into thinking that the painting you've just bought has any chance of making it ot the National Gallery, though even if you see nothing worthwhile, you can always buy hamburgers, fish and chips, chop suey or a curry from the food stalls and watch the scene as you munch away. If its wet, wear gumboots. Underfoot it can be as muddy as a farmyard.

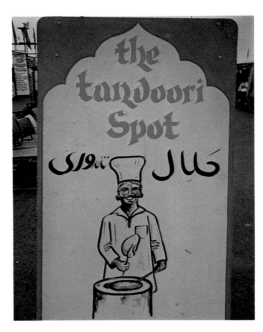

Eating out in Edinburgh can vary from traditional Scottish dishes (there's more to Scottish cuisine than the familiar haggis, smoked salmon and mutton pies and it's well worth tasting) to French (echoes of the 'Auld Alliance'), Italian, German, Indian, Mexican, Chinese and Japanese. There are dozens of cafés, usually Italian, and tearooms where genteel ladies gather around the cake stands, plush hotel restaurants, fish-and-chip shops and the well-known winter hot-dog stand and summer ice-cream vans at the bottom of the Mound. Or you can settle for a 'pie and a pint' in any bar. They're open all day.

Opposite page:
Top left: *1930s lettering adds a nice touch to this café.*
Top right: *Café in the City Art Centre in Market Street. 'Did you like the exhibition, Jean?' 'Oh, the stuff they call art nowadays . . . I wouldn't give it house-room . . . the wall here's much nicer.'*
Bottom left: *'Ah . . . you like a da posters. I put them up after the festival . . . best time of year you know . . . tourists ask me to translate . . . eez diz da way to da Castle – Spanish, Portuguese –*

I'm Scottish . . . but a wee bit Italian.'
Bottom right: *Faded 1930s décor in the Maybury Roadhouse. It's like being inside an ocean liner.*

This page:
Top left: *The domed restaurant in the George Hotel (1879), once the business office of the Caledonian Insurance Company.*
Top: *Bianco's was once a bland building society*

branch. *Re-fitting the interior revealed hidden wood panelling, stained-glass and a parquet floor. Bianco's added the stalactite chandeliers and the wall mirrors, giving the place a stylish, perhaps fortuitous look of turn-of-the-century Vienna meets Art Deco.*

Above: *The gaily painted hot-dog stand on the Mound.*

Edinburgh is Scotland's main brewing centre. For proof of this you only have to sniff the air which is often heavy with the bittersweet aroma of hops and yeast. The city has many sources of liquid refreshment – to the despair of some worthy citizens. A recent letter in the *Evening News* claimed that some of the city's bars were 'a source of great irritation and ought to be confined to desert islands and mountain tops'. In the 19th century criticism of this sort prompted publicans to transform dismal drinking dens into 'peoples palaces' to attract more respectable patronage. Some of these Victorian bars survive, in some cases perfectly preserved, and they display décor of stunning opulence.

In Ryries Bar, Haymarket (top right), stained-glass windows advertise its trade. The Café Royal's interior in West Register Street dates from 1900. The Oyster Bar (top) has a marble-topped long bar, splendid stained-glass windows showing gentlemanly Edwardian sporting pursuits and some Doulton tiled panels, one showing a Cunard steamship from the heyday of Clyde shipbuilding. In the adjacent Circle Bar (left) slender, scalloped columns support an elaborate moulded ceiling. There's a huge octagonal island bar with lamps on miniature brass Corinthian columns, mirrors, walnut screens, a marble floor and more Doulton tile pictures of famous inventors.

The 1891 interior of Bennet's Bar (right) in Leven Street is equally elaborate – intricately-carved woodwork, stained-glass windows, delicately-painted tile pictures, mirrors, arches running the full length of one wall, an ornate bar and gantry and period lighting. It's like having a drink in the Palace of Versailles.

A pot-pourri of Edinburgh shop fronts and interiors. Like the city's bars, many
date from Victorian times and show the same standard of craftsmanship.
Serendipity in the streets . . .

. . . a family butcher at Haymarket since 1875, a fishmonger in Leven Street who dresses the part, an international newsagent who didn't have the South China Morning Post, hand-painted tiles and Art Deco glass in fishshops in the Royal Mile, Scotch beef on a wall in the West End, a doorway at Murrayfield which couldn't decide on a colour scheme and a shop in the Royal Mile (opposite) which did . . .

Anyone who thinks Edinburgh consists of the view from Princes Street should explore beyond that famous mile. The outer city contains leafy 1930s suburbs, parks, villages and some bleak post-war housing schemes which do not appear in the guidebooks. And there is the Victorian city of handsome stone villas and baronial tenements built for the bourgeoisie, juxtaposed with street after street of worker housing, tradesmen's tenements and shophouses.

These so-called working class areas – and Edinburgh, despite its veneer to the contrary, does have a working class – have a vigour and community spirit which is the direct descendant of the cheek-by-jowl lifestyle which existed in the medieval Old Town. The city's tenements (many of which are architecturally distinguished) look more like Glasgow than the Edinburgh the tourist usually sees. Socially the areas of which they form the fabric come closer than any others in the city to the urban hurly-burly of Edinburgh's past.

Leith Walk is the main street between Leith and Edinburgh. It is a noble but gloomy thoroughfare. Princes Street could be on another planet. Leith, once a prosperous port, has long been Edinburgh's poor relation. Tower blocks replaced bustling tenement communities as a result of planning policies which would have been quite unacceptable in Edinburgh's New Town. More enlightened views prevail today and the historic port town is seeing a remarkable revival after many years of neglect and decline. Fine old buildings are being stone-cleaned and converted for new uses, particularly as apartments or for use by small businesses. Traditional industries are being encouraged to remain in the town.

Top left: *Bourgeois tenements marching through Marchmont. Unlike the plain if well-proportioned workers' tenements, the designs for Edinburgh's (and Glasgow's) aspiring Victorian middle-classes reflected the social pretentions of their era. The buildings shown here assume a baronial guise but many other styles were employed to flatter prospective buyers.*

Left: *'More like Glasgow than the Edinburgh the tourist usually sees.' 19th-century tenements line Gorgie Road.*

Above: *Victorian tenements stride up Leith Walk towards the old Royal Observatory on Calton Hill.*

Leith was once Scotland's premier port. It still retains a blustery, sea-going, trading atmosphere redolent of the days when its sailing ships brought wine from France, sugar from the West Indies, timber from Scandinavia and port from Portugal, the latter a trade which Scottish wine merchants pioneered. Leith's street names evoke this era – Baltic Street, Madeira Place, Elbe Street, Cadiz Street – as do the 19th-century banks and shipping offices, custom house and exchange buildings near the waterfront in Bernard Street.

Opposite page:
Top: *This wonderful antique barber shop in a surviving tenement in Henderson Street manages to preserve something of the Leith gone by.*
Bottom left: *Crates outside this fishmonger in Leith Walk conjure up images of the vanished herring fleets of Granton and of the Newhaven fishwives.*
Bottom right: *Valvona and Crolla, the Italian delicatessen in Leith Walk, a Santa's grotto of*

Italian food and wine. Many Italians have come to Scotland in search of work since the 19th century and the country has a large Italian community. Some were even working their way to New York but chose to settle in Glasgow. Some who worked on the Forth Railway Bridge decided to stay in Edinburgh.

This page: *Valvona and Crolla's shopfront in Elm Row, Leith Walk and The Central Bar, Leith, one of*

the finest Victorian bars in the Edinburgh area. Built in 1898 it has a lofty interior the height of a double-decker bus which is decorated from floor to ceiling with glazed ceramic tiles, stained-glass and carved wood-panelling. Standing by the horseshoe bar are two Leith dockers who I met there. They asked if I had 'came doon frae Embro the day' and consoled me with the assurance that I had finally arrived 'in the capital o' Scotland' – Leith, that is.

Bottom: *Brewer's sign outside the Boundary Bar.*
Right: *Leith's picturesque waterfront, seen here near Kings Landing, deserves to attract tourists. It won't see many in weather like this though. Ice-bound, it looks like one of the Dutch or Baltic ports its merchants used to trade with. Except for the restaurant from Canton.*
Far right: *A model steamship decorates the window of this palatial Leith shipping office.*
Below: *East of Leith, Edinburgh runs out of steam along the Portobello coastline. Portobello, named after a cottage built by a seaman who had fought the Spanish at Puerto Bello, Panama in 1739, was once a fashionable Edinburgh seaside resort. It still offers bracing walks along the promenade where Sir Walter Scott, dressed as a member of the Edinburgh Volunteer Light Dragoons, used to charge along the beach, sabre drawn, tilting at imaginary Napoleonic cavalry.*

Leith is still a working port and a major source of industrial employment—from whisky bonding and export to engineering, oil and marine services—in the Edinburgh area. It is also a fiercely independent town. For almost 90 years it was a separate burgh until amalgamated with its larger neighbour in 1920, an event which many Leithers still regret. They look at Edinburgh sideways, as if on a cruiser threatened by an ever-present battleship. They take occasional futile pot-shots at it but not at close range, a metaphor perhaps for their country's relationship with its southern neighbour. Leithers still talk of 'going up to Edinburgh' as if it was a different town and delight in telling visitors partisan tales—like the Boundary Bar in Leith Walk which had a line between the two burghs drawn across its floor, dividing the bar. After closing time in Edinburgh you could step over the line to the Leith half of the bar and continue drinking for another hour to the *chagrin* of Edinburgh's police force.

Visually and socially, Leith and Edinburgh's New Town would seem to have little in common. They don't. Except that much of the wealth which financed the New Town was created by the port's 18th-century merchant princes. From their terraced mansions in the eastern New Town on the north slope of Calton Hill they would sit with telescopes and watch the progress of their ships sailing up the Forth.

One house, built in 1796 in Charlotte Square at the western end of the New Town, preserves the salubrious lifestyle (for those who could afford it) of this era. The Georgian House has been meticulously restored by the National Trust for Scotland, and captures something of the 'upstairs, downstairs' domestic life of the time from the lavishly appointed drawing room to the kitchen and wine cellar. Stand still in the hallway and you can almost hear distant music and genteel chit-chat echoing down from a soirée in the drawing room, the soft tinkle of glasses over the dinner table or the clatter of pots and pans from the basement.

This page:
Left: *Cast-iron balconies are a distinctive and pleasing feature in the New Town giving a delicacy and patterned shadow-play to the austere Georgian façades.*
Bottom left: *Brass plaque in Charlotte Square. Brass name-plates are a common feature in the New Town. Usually they proclaim financial or legal services. This one is outside the Georgian House.*
Bottom right: *Fanlight window above a New Town doorway. A variety of fanlight designs can be discovered in the New Town and they give the uniform terraces some individuality.*
Opposite page:
Top: *Moray Place, begun in 1822, was the last large-scale Georgian development in the New Town. The style, influenced by Robert Adam's Charlotte Square façade, has become more laboured in its effort to impress prospective buyers. Massive columns and pediments point the way towards Victorian extravagance.*
Bottom left: *An elaborate fanlight.*
Bottom right: *Silver candelabra and Wedgwood in the dining room of the Georgian House await a dinner which will never be served.*

7
THE GEORGIAN HOUSE
THE NATIONAL TRUST FOR SCOTLAND

28

Built in response to the chronic overcrowding which was choking the Old Town by the mid-18th century, Edinburgh's New Town owes much to the bold decision of Lord Provost Drummond and his Council to hold a competition for its layout. This was won in 1767 by James Craig, an unknown local architect, who imposed his gridiron plan on the topography north of the Castle to great dramatic effect. Craig's plan is still more-or-less intact and his plunging perspectives down Frederick and Hanover Streets and the spectacular view of the Castle and the Old Town from Princes Street remain thrilling vistas today. Such was the enthusiasm for and prestige of the New Town that many of the most able Scottish architects practising in Edinburgh were commissioned to design its buildings. Now the subject of careful conservation, Provost Drummond's vision of 'fields covered in houses forming a splendid and magnificent city' imagined as he gazed from his belvedere in the decaying Old Town, is generally recognised as one of the finest examples of 18th-century town planning in the world.

Left: *The façade of Robert Adam's dignified terrace in Charlotte Square (1791) is outstanding among Edinburgh's many distinguished buildings.*

Above: *'... to come on a corner and see a perspective of a mile or more of falling street and beyond ... a blue arm of the sea and the hills upon the further side ...' Stevenson, who lived in the New Town was impressed by its streetscapes. This one is looking down Frederick Street. Beyond St Stephen's Church (1827) are the River Forth and the hills of Fife.*
Below: *Stevenson's children's poem 'The Lamplighter' inscribed on a plaque outside his Heriot Row home.*

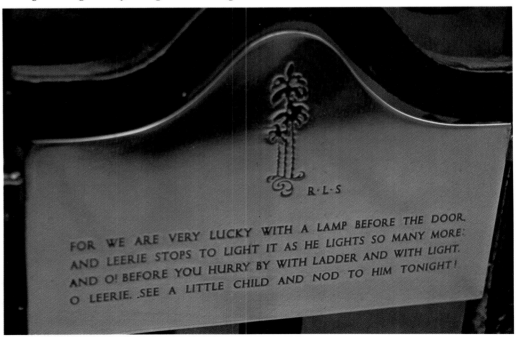

R·L·S

FOR WE ARE VERY LUCKY WITH A LAMP BEFORE THE DOOR,
AND LEERIE STOPS TO LIGHT IT AS HE LIGHTS SO MANY MORE:
AND O! BEFORE YOU HURRY BY WITH LADDER AND WITH LIGHT,
O LEERIE, SEE A LITTLE CHILD AND NOD TO HIM TONIGHT!

On the northern plain between the New Town and the sea the amazing roofline of Fettes College (1870), designed by David Bryce, dominates the skyline. Bryce designed many Victorian buildings in Edinburgh including some in the New Town but none surpass the architectural panache of this mesmeric chateau.

Of all the buildings in Edinburgh, it is the Castle which exerts the most haunting presence. Sometimes it will take you by surprise as you turn a corner or crest a hill. Often it appears at its most majestically menacing when you can hardly see it at all. Here, it looms out of the mist as you enter the city along Queensferry Road.

Top left: *George Heriot's Hospital (1659) 'one of the finest buildings of the Northern European Renaissance' framed by tombstones in Greyfriars Churchyard. Greyfriars is a mysterious, eerie place full of alarming memories. This is where the graverobbers Burke and Hare perpetrated their devilish deeds. In its church the National Covenant, resisting Charles I's 'Papist religion' was signed and subsequently over 1,000 Covenanters endured a winter of imprisonment there before being executed in the Grassmarket or banished to slavery on the plantations of Virginia. And, on a less serious note, it's where Greyfriars Bobby, the faithful Skye terrier, maintained a 14-year vigil by his master's grave–a story so sentimental that Walt Disney was moved to film it.*
Left: *The Castle from Inverleith looking like a French Impressionist painting.*
Far left: *Greyfriars Bobby at the top of Candlemaker Row.*

Above: *The Castle from Brown's Place. Nearby are the remains of the Flodden Wall, built to protect the city from a potential English invasion after the Battle of Flodden in 1513. Flodden was a desperate day in Scottish history. It was the country's most calamitous military defeat. Thousands of Scots, including many Edinburgh people, perished on the battlefield along with their King, James IV. Economically and culturally, Scotland had flourished during James's enlightened reign, considered to have been something of a 'golden age' in Scottish history. Tragically, the battle need never have happened. The reason for James's invasion of England–he ventured south in support of the 'Auld Alliance'–was an Anglo/French quarrel (part of European political differences of the time) which was resolved soon afterwards, independent of any Scottish influence.*

Ghosts haunt Greyfriars Churchyard and are abroad in the Old Town too. Deacon Brodie, an eminent councillor by day, was a notorious burglar by night. He went to the gallows in the 18th century but is his spectre still floating around? Does Rabbie Burns still haunt the White Hart Inn and where is that piper playing his echoing lament? What family secrets does the bric-a-brac in the antique shops hold? In the evening, when a sudden, enigmatic hush envelopes its wynds and closes, Edinburgh's Old Town becomes the medieval labyrinth it once was. A town of ambush and brief swordfights, anguished cries in the dark and clattering footsteps escaping down cobbled alleys, family vendettas and Machiavellian intrigue whispered beneath the laughter in countless bawdy bars. And by day, a precipitous hill town, awake to cacophonous squalour, washed by the weather, bombarded by cannon, yet prosperous and enobled by the glower of its kirk and ancient citadel.

Far left: *Like an Expressionist film set, buildings in Victoria Street sweep down towards the Grassmarket, an area of bagpipe-makers and antique shops.*
Left: *Clattering footsteps break the enigmatic hush which envelopes the Old Town's wynds and closes.*

*Edinburgh Castle floodlit at night looms above a
deserted Grassmarket.*

Edinburgh's unmistakable city centre panorama – the world-famous view looking west from the North British Hotel. It has as many moods as ways in which it is reproduced – on everything from picture postcards to shortbread tins.

From left to right: *The Victorian steeple of Tolbooth St John's Church (1844) and the dome of the Bank of Scotland (1870) on the skyline of the Old Town, the spires of the Church of Scotland's New College and Assembly Hall (1850) and Edinburgh Castle. Below Castle Rock are the sunken railway approach to Waverley Station (1848), the Greek style National Gallery of Scotland (1845) and the Royal Scottish Academy (1832) on the Mound. At the far end of Princes Street are the Caledonian Hotel (1903), the Venetian campanile of St George's West Church (1869), the spires (1917) of St Mary's Episcopal Cathedral and the dome of West Register House (1811) in Charlotte Square. In the foreground is the Gothic Scott Monument (1844) in Princes Street Gardens.*

Evening lights begin to twinkle on Princes Street as the famous view disappears with the daylight—the magic twilight hour—evoking Stevenson's memorable sentiment 'there are no stars so lovely as Edinburgh street lamps'.

Shopfront near Tollcross

Picture credits: *All photographs are by Robin Ward except as follows:* Page 24 (top) Edinburgh City Libraries, (bottom) National Portrait Gallery. Page 25 (top) *The Scotsman,* (bottom) National Portrait Gallery. Page 38 (top and bottom) Edinburgh City Libraries. Page 39 (top) Edinburgh City Libraries, (bottom) *The Scotsman.* Page 46 Scottish Record Office. Page 54 Edinburgh Military Tattoo. Page 55 (bottom) Scottish Tourist Board. Page 58 (painting) National Gallery of Modern Art. Page 59 (paintings) National Gallery of Scotland.

Special thanks are due to National Galleries of Scotland for permission to photograph their collections, and to the many people and institutions in the city who were helpful in the preparation of this book.